U.S. Census
A Mirror of America

Ruth Kassinger

RSVP

RAINTREE
STECK-VAUGHN
P U B L I S H E R S
A Steck-Vaughn Company

Austin, Texas
www.steck-vaughn.com

To Anna, Austen, and Alice

Published by Raintree Steck-Vaughn Publishers, an imprint of the Steck-Vaughn Company

Publishing Director: Walter Kossmann
Editor: Shirley Shalit
Design Project Managers: Lyda Guz and Richard Dooley
Photo Research: Margie Foster

Photo Credits: Cover and pp. 4t, 11, 18, 24t, 31, 39t, 46, 54, 59, 66 © Den Fisher/Tony Stone International. p. 4b © Douglas Borrows/Gamma-Liaison; p. 6 (both) Park Street; p. 7 Library of Congress; p. 9 © PhotoDisc; p. 12 AP/Wide World; p. 16 Corbis/Hulton Deutsch Collection; p. 19 Courtesy of Crane Museum, Dalton, MA; pp. 20, 22, 23 National Archives; p. 24b Missouri Historical Society; p. 25 MapQuest.Com, Inc.; p. 27 The Granger Collection, New York; p. 32 (both) National Portrait Gallery, Smithsonian Institution; p. 35 National Archives; p. 37 The Granger Collection, New York; p. 38 North Wind Picture Archives; p. 39b Corbis; p. 40 © PhotoDisc; p. 42 The Granger Collection, New York; p. 43 North Wind Picture Archives; p. 47 The Granger Collection, New York; p. 48 Library of Congress; p. 49 (both) National Portrait Gallery, Smithsonian Institution; p. 51 Brown Brothers; p. 52 The Granger Collection, New York; pp. 55 (both), 57 Corbis/Bettmann; p. 58 Brown Brothers; p. 62 Corbis; p. 63 Corbis/Flip Schulke; p. 65 North Carolina General Assembly; p. 67 Corbis/Bettmann; p. 69 Corbis/Seattle Post-Intelligencer Collection; p. 70 Corbis/AFP; p. 74 U.S. Census Bureau.

Library of Congress Cataloging-in-Publication Data
Kassinger, Ruth
    U.S. census: a mirror of America / Ruth Kassinger.
        p.   cm.
    Includes bibliographical references and index.
    Summary: Recounts the history of the census in the United States from the eighteenth century to the present and describes the methods used to take it and how they have changed.
    ISBN 0-7398-1217-3
    1. United States — Census — History Juvenile literature.   2. United States — Census — Methodology Juvenile literature. [1. United States — Census.] I. Title. II Title: US census.
HA181. K37 1999   99-25015
304.6'07'23 — dc21   CIP

Printed and bound in Mexico.
1 2 3 4 5 6 7 8 9 0 RRD 03 02 01 00 99

Contents

1

How to Take a Census

Start with Three Million Pencils....

One day in late March 2000 your family, like every other family in America, will find a large, white envelope in the mailbox. Inside the envelope will be the 2000 census questionnaire from the U.S. Bureau of the Census and instructions on how to fill it out. When your family completes the questionnaire, you will be participating in the U.S. census, the oldest continuing census in the world.

What is the U.S. census? It is the count we take once every ten years of the people living in America. The count (also called the *enumeration*, which means "numbering") takes place on a particular day in every year ending with a "0." This coming Census Day

The U.S. Census counts people where they live. Some people do not live in houses or apartments and are hard to find. In 1990, the Census Bureau chose one night to count the homeless. Census takers searched under bridges, in shelters, and in bus depots and train yards to find them.

is April 1, 2000. A *decennial* (every ten years) census is required by our Constitution. The first census was in 1790. The 2000 census will be the 22nd census of the American people.

In 2000, the Census Bureau expects to count approximately 275 million people. What does it take to count 275 million people? It takes a lot of people—over 500,000 Census Bureau workers. It also takes more than three million pencils, and six tractor-trailer trucks of paper clips. It also costs a bundle: The 2000 census will cost about $5–$7 billion, which means $18–$25 for every person counted.

Finding the People

Making sure everyone in the country is counted is a difficult job. In the United States, we count people at their homes. The Census Bureau tries to make sure everyone is counted once—and only once—by linking everyone to one home address. The Bureau, which is part of the U.S. Department of Commerce, sends a census questionnaire to every household address in the United States. The questionnaire isn't addressed to particular people. Everybody who lives at the address includes his or her information on the questionnaire.

How does the Bureau know all the home addresses? The Bureau's address list for 2000 is based on its 1990 address list plus information provided by the U.S. Postal Service. The Bureau also sends out its employees to make sure addresses are still accurate and to scout out new residences. Since new houses and apartment buildings are always being built, old buildings are

Help from the Post Office

You might think that the Bureau could just use a list of addresses from the Post Office. But until recently, the U.S. Postal Service, in order to protect people's privacy, was not allowed to share its list. Also, the Postal Service lists mix business and home addresses. And some people have their mail delivered to more than one address or to post office boxes, not to their houses.

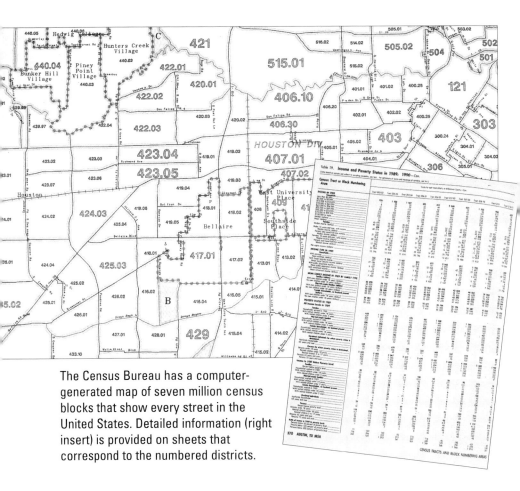

The Census Bureau has a computer-generated map of seven million census blocks that show every street in the United States. Detailed information (right insert) is provided on sheets that correspond to the numbered districts.

being torn down, and sometimes warehouse space is being turned into living space, an actual check is often needed. As the Bureau gets information, it updates its seven million detailed, computerized maps that display every street in the country.

One of the difficulties with taking a census in America is that Americans move often. About 17 percent of us change addresses each year. Also, some people, like college students, retired people, and children who live with divorced parents, have more than one address. Some people, like those who live in recreational vehicles or on boats, don't have a fixed address. Some people, called the homeless, have no address at all. These are challenges for the Census Bureau.

Asking the Questions

Most people will get a "short form" questionnaire with these seven questions:

1. What is this person's name?
2. What is this person's telephone number?
3. What is this person's sex?
4. What is this person's age and what is this person's date of birth?
5. Is this person Spanish/Hispanic/Latino?
6. What is this person's race?
7. What is this person's marital status?

One out of every six households will get a "long form" questionnaire with 46 additional questions. The long form includes questions about the kind and value of the home the family lives in, how family members get to work, and what the adults do for a living and how much they get paid. (You can find the long form in the Appendix at the back of this book.)

Until 1960, *enumerators* (the people whose job it is to actually take the count) went to every home to ask people the census questions and write down their responses. (In the early decades of America's history, many people couldn't read or write and had to rely on the enumerators' help.) In 1960, the Census Bureau mailed questionnaires to households and enumerators picked up

Our modern "mail-back" questionnaire gives people more privacy than people had in 1870 (shown here). Also, in the 1950s, the Census Bureau discovered that a significant portion of the errors in the census was due to "enumerator error." The Bureau found the enumerators accurately wrote down the answers to simple questions like age and sex, but made mistakes when they wrote down the answers to questions about occupation and industry.

7

the completed forms. Since 1970, the Census Bureau has mailed a census questionnaire to every household, with instructions to mail the questionnaire back. This "mail-back" system is a much less expensive and more private way to take the census.

Unfortunately, some people do not send their questionnaires back. When that happens, the Bureau has to send an enumerator to each address that has not responded. The enumerators work with the residents to fill out the form.

Other countries use different methods to count their people. In some countries, like China, everyone has to let the government know every time they move. It is easy to take a census in China because the government always knows where everyone is. The government of Turkey used a different method when it took a census in 1997. Everyone in Turkey was required to stay home for 14 hours, so census takers could go house-to-house and count. Neither one of these methods would be acceptable to Americans, however. We have a tradition of privacy and a dislike of government intrusion that would make the methods of China and Turkey impossible.

What Happens to the Information?

As you will see in the next chapter, the most important use of the census *data* (facts or information) is to determine how many members of the House of Representatives each state sends to Washington, D.C. The greater the population of a state, the greater the state's share of representatives in Congress is. But from the very first census, we have used the information for other purposes.

The U.S. government (which is also called the *federal government*) collects taxes from all the country's citizens. Part of that money is used to pay for programs that benefit the people. The federal government funds programs that build highways, provide food stamps so poor families can buy food, and support school programs like Headstart, which helps preschoolers get ready for elementary school. The federal government often passes along the money to states to further distribute. Both the federal government and state

National Archives Building

Information from the census is available to everyone. Don't worry, though: The information is not available by name or address! No one can find out the answers that you or your family write down until 72 years have passed. The answers from your family are *aggregated* (mixed in and totaled) with the answers from other people in your particular area and only the totals for the area are available to the public. After 72 years, the census records go to the National Archives and become available to researchers. You can visit the National Archives in Washington, D.C. and look up your ancestors' census data.

governments use census data to properly distribute billions of dollars for government programs.

State and county or city governments also use the census data to plan for the future. Census data, for example, may show that a lot of babies were born in your county in the last few years. Your county government may decide to build a new elementary school now because it knows that in a few years those babies will be ready for kindergarten.

Businesses find the census information very useful. Let's say a magazine publisher wants to mail free copies of a Spanish language magazine to people who might like it and want to buy a *subscription*. The publisher could use census data to identify neighborhoods that have a high proportion of Spanish-speaking people. Or, maybe you want to open a nursing home in Omaha, Nebraska, but don't know exactly where. You might use census data to see which neighborhoods have a large population of older people.

Historians and other scholars also find census data very useful. They know that understanding how our population changed over time can help explain why certain events happened in our history. In the late 1800s and early 1900s, for example, millions of very poor immigrants from eastern and central Europe settled in America's cities. The poverty, crowding, and crime of the big cities deepened prejudices against immigrants and eventually led Congress to vote to limit immigration in 1920.

The U.S. census results reflect many changes in America over the course of our history. You will see how in 210 years America transformed itself from a nation of four million farmers clustered along the Atlantic Ocean into an industrial nation of almost 275 million people. You will discover how America, once dominated by people of northern European heritage, became a nation of people whose ancestors come from around the globe.

You will also see how the changes in census-taking itself reveal the story of America. (For example, the census didn't count most Native Americans until 1890: What does this say about what most Americans in the 19th century thought of Native Americans?) To see all these changes, though, we need to go all the way back to the beginning of our nation, to 1789, which was the year that Thomas Jefferson, George Washington, John Adams, James Madison, and other "founding fathers" wrote the U.S. Constitution.

2

Why Take the Census?

Choosing Teams for the Game of Government

In 1776, the 13 American colonies declared their independence from Great Britain. In 1781, the new states agreed to form a national government under a document called the Articles of Confederation. Two years later, in 1783, the American War of Independence from Britain ended and the United States of America was born. The national government under the Articles of Confederation, however, was not working well, and in the summer of 1787, delegates from the 13 states met in Philadelphia to change and improve the Articles. Instead of revising them, however, the delegates wrote an entirely new document: the Constitution of the United States.

The Constitution was a unique document establishing a new form of government that the world had never seen before. One of the most important new ideas in the Constitution was that the government would be representative of the population by means of elections. One of the most interesting parts of the Constitution was how it made the government representative.

Deciding How to Make the Government Representative

Under the Articles of Confederation, all states had one representative to Congress. Large states were unhappy with this: They felt they should have more representatives because they had more individuals

Selecting Senators

The Constitution provided for direct election by the people of members of the House of Representatives. The Constitution had a more traditional method for selecting senators: They were chosen by the states' legislatures. Not until 1913 was the Constitution amended to provide for direct election of senators.

to represent. But small states feared that their citizens' interests would be ignored if large states had more representatives than they did.

To solve this problem, the authors of the Constitution (who are sometimes called the *framers*) established two legislative, or law-making, bodies: the Senate and the House of Representatives. In the Senate, every state is represented by two senators, regardless of the size of the state. Today this means that Delaware with a population of about 730,000 has the same number of senators as California with a population of more than 32 million. In the Senate, the interests of each state are equally represented.

In the House of Representatives, however, the members are *apportioned* (meaning "distributed" or "divided and shared out") according to the population of each state. In the House of Representatives, states with large populations have a greater number of Representatives—and therefore votes—than states with smaller populations. This is why today California has 52 Representatives and Delaware has 1.

The number of members of the House of Representatives grew as the country's population grew. There were 106 members in 1790, and seats were added each decade as the country's population increased until 1910. After 1910, Congress decided that the size of the House threatened to become unwieldy and limited the numbers of its members to its current level, 435.

In the House, the interests of each individual are equally represented. In 1790, there were 106 representatives—roughly one for every 30,000 people. Today, there are 435 members of the House of Representatives. That means each representative represents about 630,000 people.

The Essential Census

It would be impossible for our representative system to work without knowing how many people there are to represent. So, right in the first Article of the Constitution is the requirement for a census. The language of 1787 is a little hard to understand today, so here is the original, followed by a version in today's language:

The 1787 original:
Representatives and direct Taxes shall be apportioned among the several States which may be included within this Union, according to their respective Numbers, which shall be determined by adding to the whole Number of free Persons, including those bound to Service for a Term of Years, and excluding Indians not taxed, three fifths of all other Persons. The actual Enumeration shall be made within three Years after the first Meeting of the Congress of the United States, and within every subsequent Term of ten Years, in such Manner as they shall by Law direct.

A version in today's language:
States will have a number of representatives and owe taxes to the federal government according to how many people live in each state. A census of the people will be taken by 1790 and every ten years thereafter. In the census a free person (which means *indentured servants*, too) will count as one person and a slave will count as three-fifths of a person. Because Indians don't pay taxes, they won't count at all, unless they live as members of the white community.

13

The framers of the Constitution knew that the American population would grow and people would move from place to place between censuses. So, they required Congress to conduct a census and make a new apportionment of representatives every ten years. After every census for the past 200 years, each state's number of representatives has been reconsidered and sometimes changed, depending on the number of people in the state as revealed by the last census. When a new apportionment is made, it is called a *reapportionment*.

Taxes

You may notice that the framers wrote that the census would have two purposes. It would be used not only to apportion representatives, but also to apportion taxes. Today the census has nothing to do with taxes: The government raises most of its funds from taxes on individuals' or businesses' income. In fact, Congress only passed laws twice (in 1798 and during the War of 1812) to apportion a national tax. Why did the framers link taxes and the census in the Constitution in 1787?

The federal government was in trouble in 1787. Under the Articles of Confederation, the federal government didn't have any power to raise money. This was a major problem because, although the states promised to send money based on the value of land in each state, many did not live up to their promises.

Under the Constitution the federal government gained the power to tax. The framers thought it would be fair to divide the debts equally among the people, and so they wrote into the Constitution a link between taxes and the census results. The framers also suspected that states might be tempted to cheat about the number of people living in the state because the Constitution provided that more people meant more representatives. More representatives meant more political power. If however, more people also meant paying more taxes, then the states would be less tempted to boost their population count.

States' Honesty

There was good reason to think there might be some cheating by the states in the census. The Articles of Confederation called for an apportionment among the states of national expenses based on the population of the states. By 1783, only the small states of New Hampshire, Rhode Island, Connecticut, and Delaware had taken any sort of census. By 1787, every state had estimated its population, but all states except Georgia considerably underestimated their populations. The total undercount among the states was more than half a million (out of a total of about four million).

Slaves and Indians

Another thing you surely noticed about the census language in the Constitution is that a slave counted as only three-fifths of a person. Slavery was a national issue right from the earliest days of the nation. In 1787, delegates from the Northern and Southern states debated at length whether slaves should be counted in the census and how they should be counted: Were they property that should not be counted or people who should be fully counted? The framers finally compromised on counting slaves as three-fifths of a person to encourage the Southern, slaveholding states to approve the new Constitution. Delegates from the Southern states wanted to count slaves fully—despite the fact that slaves were considered mere property and had no rights at all—because counting slaves would give the Southern states a greater census population and more power in Congress.

There was little talk among the delegates in 1787 about how the Native Americans (who are also known as Indians) were to be counted in the census. Delegates agreed that Indians were not to be counted for purposes of apportionment and representation in the government. The phrase "excluding Indians not taxed" was a statement meant to exclude any Indians except those few living and working in the white community. Only those living among the whites would be subject to *excise taxes* (taxes on the manufacture

Counting the Native Americans

No one knows exactly how many Native Americans were in North America when the first colonists from Europe arrived. About one million is a good guess. The Indian population fell fast between 1800 and 1850. Disease brought by the European immigrants and death from starvation and war devastated Native Americans. It is estimated that only about 250,000 Native Americans were left in the United States by 1850.

Until 1860, Native Americans were not counted separately in any census. In the censuses of 1860, 1870, and 1880, there was a count of "Indians taxed," but the numbers are not considered accurate. (The count of Indians taxed increased from about 26,000 to 66,000 between 1870 and 1880. That large an increase in ten years tells us that one or both of the figures were inaccurate.) Part of the problem was a question of definition: Who counted as an Indian? Since it was up to the enumerators to decide by observing the people in the household, the count of Native Americans could (and did!) vary considerably.

In 1890, the Census Bureau enumerators attempted to count all Native Americans for the first time. However, they still were instructed to distinguish between Indians taxed and not taxed. Indians "living on reservations" or "roaming individually, or in bands, over unsettled tracts of the country" were classified as Indians not taxed. This meant the Native Americans living outside the white community still were not counted for purposes of representation in Congress. This approach was terribly unfair because in the 19th century Congress made laws

A Plains Indians family, 1880s.

and approved treaties that affected Native Americans in basic ways—such as taking away their traditional lands and creating reservations for them. Finally, in 1935, a Supreme Court case determined there were no longer any "Indians not taxed" in the United States. In 1940, for the first time, all Native Americans were counted for apportionment.

or sale of goods) and property taxes, which were the taxes people of the time were most likely to have to pay.

The Civil War and the Thirteenth Amendment to the Constitution abolished slavery in 1865. The Fourteenth Amendment to the Constitution became law in 1868 and officially ended the three-fifths rule. The exclusion from the census of "Indians not taxed" is still a part of the Constitution, but as of the 1940 census, all Native Americans were considered to be taxed and were counted. Today the Census Bureau aims to count everyone resident in this country (as well as American diplomats and military personnel overseas) on Census Day. Only foreign tourists and foreign diplomats are excluded.

Taking the First Census

The Constitution required that the first census be taken by 1790. Deciding to take a census, however, and actually taking one were two different things. The very existence of the government, though, depended on it.

3

The First Census

1790

In 1790, three years after the Constitution was signed, Congress prepared for the first census. The Constitution required that the government count the people, but it didn't say how to do it. The Constitution said that it was up to Congress to decide how to do the counting.

Congress chose to direct the U.S. Marshals to do the job. For more than a century after 1789, the Marshals were the only nationwide police power available to the president, Congress, and the courts to enforce the laws made by the United States government. There were 17 Marshals in 1790 and they hired about 650 assistants to help take the census. The Marshals and their assistants were the census enumerators, the people who do the counting.

Congress gave the Marshals nine months to count everyone in the country. What Congress didn't give them, though, were pens and paper. Paper was scarce and more expensive than it is today (although pens made out of feather quills were easy to come by), and so they had to use whatever scraps of paper they could find!

Problems

In 1790 there were 13 colonies covering almost one million square miles. Congress knew it was going to be a hard job to count everyone. About 95 percent of Americans lived on farms. There were only a few cities where enumerators could quickly find

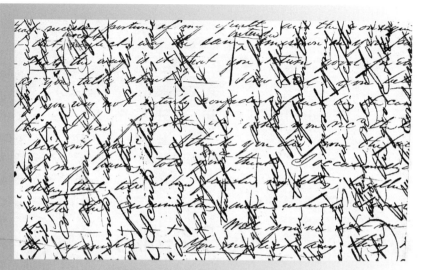

Using Scarce Paper

Paper was truly scarce in the early United States. People went to great lengths to fully use pieces of paper, as you can see from this letter which has been written on twice. Much of the paper Americans had used before the War of Independence had been imported from Britain. There were a few American producers of paper (which, like all paper of the time, was made from old rags), but most of the supply was already committed to newspapers and the few book publishers in business. During the Revolutionary War, paper for rifle cartridges was so scarce that the army used pages from a supply of unshipped Bibles for the purpose.

people. (New York, the second biggest city after Philadelphia, had only about 50,000 inhabitants—compared to seven million today.)

Most of the nation was sparsely settled. There were often miles between houses in the countryside and on the frontier. An enumerator, traveling on horseback from farm to farm, could take all day to count a few dozen people. To encourage the enumerators to make the effort to find everyone, Congress paid them for each person counted. They got one dollar for every 300 persons counted in cities of over 5,000 people, two dollars for every 300 people counted in country areas, and six dollars for 300 people counted in frontier areas.

19

A map of population density in the 13 original states demonstrating how sparsely populated the country was.

It was no wonder enumerators were better paid for counting people who lived outside the cities: Getting from one farm to another in America of 1790 was difficult. No one had invented asphalt, the "blacktop" we use to surface most of our roads with today, and there were no concrete highways. With luck, a traveler between cities might find stretches of "corduroy" road, which was road made of short lengths of logs laid side-by-side across the route. (You can imagine how uncomfortable it would have been to travel in a carriage with iron-rimmed wooden wheels—and no shock absorbers—over a stretch of corduroy road!) Enumerators traveling miles between farms, however, would find only dirt roads or trails, which were often treacherous with mud or ice. At the end of a day, they would be lucky to find an inn where they could sleep for the night.

People were not always willing to give information to the enumerators. In our modern world, we are used to filling out forms. All kinds of organizations collect information from us. Today, health insurance companies, for example, gather information about our health, and schools conduct statewide tests and collect information about our education. Tax agencies of federal, state, and local governments ask us for information about how much we earn and how we spend our earnings. Doctors and hospitals are required to report when we come down with certain diseases.

In the late 1700s in America, though, there was little tradition of information gathering. Towns and colonies sometimes would try to take a count of their populations, but not on a regular basis. Churches kept track of births, marriages, and deaths, but usually only those of their own members. No organizations gathered information on a national scale. So, not everyone cooperated when the census enumerators came in 1790 to count the members of their families. Even the six simple questions on the first census made some people feel that the government was invading their privacy.

The Census Questions in 1790

When an enumerator arrived at a house in 1790, he asked the head of the family six questions:

1. What is your name?
2. How many free white males over 16 live here?
3. How many free white males under 16 live here?
4. How many free white females live here?
5. How many slaves live here?
6. How many other free persons live here?

Today, the census gathers information about each individual in the family. But from 1790 until 1850 the census just asked for totals from the head of the household.

Why didn't the census have just one question: How many people live here? Remember that slaves had to be counted separately because the Constitution said they counted for only three-fifths of a person in the census. The Constitution also said to count Indians only if they lived in the white community. The question about "other free persons" would identify Indians, as well as any free blacks. Finally, conflicts with foreign countries and Native American tribes convinced Congress it would be a good idea to find out how many Americans could fight in a war. So Congress also inquired about the number of free males who were older than 16 (and therefore could be called to fight).

The American Family

In one way, it was easier to count people in 1790 than it is today. Today people live in many different kinds of places: in recreational vehicles, on sailboats, in college dorms, and in nursing homes or hospitals. Young adults, especially in cities, may move often. The homeless have no permanent address at all. Today, it is hard to find some people or decide where they should be counted.

The word "family" had a broader definition in 1790 than it does today. Members of a family were not just relatives by blood or marriage. Slaves, servants, and *apprentices* who lived in the same house (or in slave quarters or other housing on the same property) were considered members of that family. In the 1700s, almost everyone lived in a family and nearly every family lived in a house, whether in a city, town, or on a farm. If enumerators could visit all the houses, they would find all the families—and therefore all the people!

There were few places other than houses where people could live. There were no nursing homes. Older people who were unable to live in their own homes moved into the home of a relative. There were few hospitals; sick people were usually cared for at home. There were no homeless people. If a person could not afford a home and had no family, the town or church would pay to lodge that person with another family in the town.

Grown children generally did not move out on their own until they were married and could build or buy their own house. Apprentices had to finish their apprenticeships, and indentured servants had to finish their *indentures*, (the years

These are the results of the 1790 Census. Thomas Jefferson, who was secretary of state, signed the document.

of labor that they had promised in exchange for passage by ship to America) before they could marry and move out of their "family." There were only a few colleges. Even the college students often lived with local families.

The Results of the 1790 Census

After the enumerators counted the people in their areas, they posted a list of all the families and their census answers in two public places in each area. Everyone could look at the list and report any mistakes. It took 18 months to complete the census. The total number of people living in America came to 3,893,637, of whom 18 percent were slaves.

President George Washington and other government leaders thought the count was too low—and they were undoubtedly right. President Washington decided that the census was accurate enough to be used to apportion Congress, but he and other leaders were disappointed in the census total. England, France, and Spain had colonies in North America. These countries' interests were often opposed to American interests. American leaders wanted higher population figures so they could demonstrate that the United States was a rapidly growing country and a power that should be taken seriously. The next decades would prove them right.

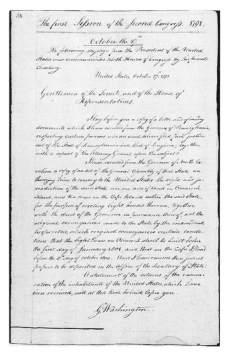

President George Washington agreed that the census results were good enough to accept, although he and others knew that not everyone had been counted. Even today, with all of modern technology, the census does not count everyone. The 1990 census failed to count 9.7 million people and counted 4.4 million people twice.

4

"A Wonder to Ourselves!"
America and the Census
from 1800–1850

America Grows

In 1800, the United States of America had been independent from Britain for only 17 years. The 13 original states plus the three new ones—Vermont, Kentucky, and Tennessee—were situated along the Atlantic Ocean and in the Appalachian Mountains. Altogether, America covered 891,000 square miles, about one-quarter of its current size. Native American tribes, Spain, Britain, and France claimed the rest of the North American continent. Only about five million people—many fewer than live in

As President, Thomas Jefferson sent a team of explorers headed by Meriwether Lewis and William Clark to explore the Louisiana Purchase and to see if it was possible to navigate rivers from the Mississippi to the Pacific Ocean. Lewis and Clark recorded events and drew animals they encountered, such as this sage grouse, in a journal that they kept during their journey.

24

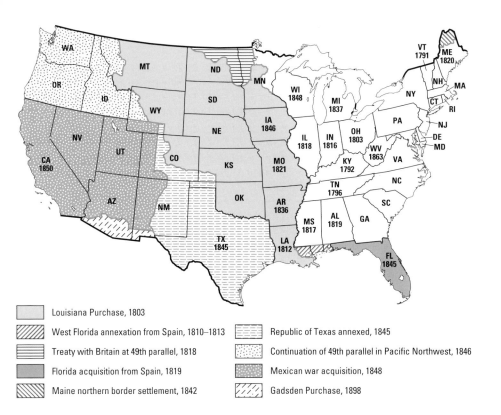

Louisiana Purchase, 1803

West Florida annexation from Spain, 1810–1813

Treaty with Britain at 49th parallel, 1818

Florida acquisition from Spain, 1819

Maine northern border settlement, 1842

Republic of Texas annexed, 1845

Continuation of 49th parallel in Pacific Northwest, 1846

Mexican war acquisition, 1848

Gadsden Purchase, 1898

Map of the United States showing the additions of territory from the Louisiana Purchase to the acquisition of the Pacific Northwest.

New York City today—lived in all of America. Eighty percent of Americans lived east of the Appalachian Mountains.

The U.S. doubled its size in 1803 to 1.7 million square miles when it purchased the Louisiana Territory—stretching from the Mississippi River to the Rocky Mountains and from the Gulf of Mexico to Canada—from the French. Then, in the next decades, the U.S. added more territory by forcing Native American people to give up their traditional lands. In 1819, Florida was acquired from Spain. After the defeat of Mexico in the war of 1845, Texas and the vast California territory in the southwest were added. In 1846, the U.S. came to an agreement with Britain and gained the northwest land that would become Washington, Oregon, Idaho, and parts of Montana and Wyoming.

The result was that by 1850, America covered nearly 3 million square miles of land and had spread across the continent from the

Atlantic to the Pacific Ocean. Fifteen new states had been formed from the new territories. The states included ones in the farthest reaches of the country: Maine, Florida, and California.

The American population was growing fast, too, particularly in the new western territories. The population of Ohio, for example, grew more than fourfold between 1810 and 1830. By 1850, the number of Americans had grown to 23 million—about four and a half times the number in 1800. America had more people than Britain, its former colonial ruler.

Some of the rapid increase in population resulted from the fact that American women in the early 1800s married early and therefore had more years in which to have children. Also, most Americans lived in the countryside, which was a healthy place to live. They were likely to have fresh vegetables to eat and milk to drink. (The 1850 census showed Americans owned 6,485,094 milk cows.) Rural Americans were less likely to die from diseases like tuberculosis, typhoid, and cholera that spread quickly through cities. In addition, immigrants kept arriving from Europe: 2.5 million came between 1820 and 1850. When Wisconsin became a state in 1848, nearly one-third of its citizens were immigrants, largely from Germany and the Scandinavian countries.

The Census Expands

Since the early days of independence, Thomas Jefferson, James Madison, and other leading thinkers had argued for using the census to gather more data than a simple count of Americans. They proposed that the census collect economic information and more detailed information about the population. Congress wasn't convinced and thought of the census solely as a means of apportioning the seats in the House of Representatives. It authorized the same six census questions that it had in 1790. A frustrated Madison wrote to Jefferson that Congress apparently thought a more detailed census was just "a waste of trouble and supplying materials for idle people to make a book."

By the 1810 census, however, Congress changed its mind. It forged a new direction for the decennial census as the means to gather a multitude of details about the American population and economy. The objective of the census was greatly expanded.

What inspired this change? In 1803, Britain and France went to war. The war was fought with rifles, warships, and cannons, but also with trade regulations. Each side was determined to punish the other by preventing its opponent from buying and from selling goods to foreign countries. Britain, with its great navy, blockaded the ports of France and forbade ships of any nation from landing. The French prohibited all countries from complying with the British trade regulations.

The United States had been trading with both countries, exporting raw materials like tobacco, rice, and whale oil, and importing manufactured goods. U.S. merchants shipping goods overseas were

British Impressment

During their war with France, the British not only seized American ships, they also seized sailors who manned the ships. The practice was called impressment and it was Britain's way of adding sailors to the Royal Navy. British law allowed the commanders of warships to draft able-bodied British subjects wherever they found them. So, when the British stopped American ships, they looked for deserters from the British Navy. The British weren't very particular, however, and took British-born sailors who had become naturalized U.S. citizens, as well as some native-born Americans.

suddenly in a terrible position. Both Britain and France seized U.S. ships for breaking their laws. Between 1804 and 1807, the British seized 1,000 American ships and the French took about 500.

President Thomas Jefferson was determined not to go to war against either country, despite their unreasonable actions. He thought he could avoid war and convince the French and British to leave U.S. ships alone by denying them American raw materials. At his urging, Congress passed the Embargo Act in December 1807. The Act prohibited all American ships from leaving American ports for foreign destinations.

The Embargo Act failed. American farmers watched their products pile up at the wharves. American merchants saw their ships lying idle in the harbors. Neither France nor Britain changed its policies. American shippers and farmers were losing money. They were furious and persuaded Congress to *repeal* the Embargo Act in 1809.

One of the lessons that some Americans drew from the experience of the Embargo Act was that the United States was too dependent on exporting raw materials and importing finished products from Europe. If the nation was to be independent of European problems, it needed to be more self-sufficient. It needed a more balanced economy.

Thomas Jefferson Sets the Record Straight

As ambassador to France, Thomas Jefferson, who would later become our third president, worked hard to educate the French about his beloved country. When a leading French naturalist, Georges de Buffon, declared that the animals of North America were smaller than those in Europe, Jefferson was determined to prove him wrong. He sent an expedition, at his own expense, to New Hampshire to collect and send him specimens.

One day a huge crate with an odd odor and a return address of New Hampshire arrived at Jefferson's Paris home. Inside was a dead—and not very well preserved—moose. Jefferson displayed it anyhow, smelly and balding, in his front hall. It was a small sacrifice to make for setting the record straight about America.

If, as President Jefferson hoped, manufacturing, business, agriculture, and navigation were to be "the four pillars of our prosperity," the country needed to know the strength of each of those pillars. No one was sure, however, what manufactured goods America did produce. No one was sure how many people were employed in the various occupations. So, in 1810, Congress took the census in a new direction and included a detailed accounting of manufactures. In 1820, the census asked everyone to identify whether they worked in agriculture, commerce, or manufacturing.

The census quickly took a new role in helping the government describe the economy and shape the country's economic future. By 1850, the census asked questions about the country's production at the most detailed level. In agriculture, the census asked, for example, for the quantity produced of 29 different crops, including hemp (for making rope), beeswax, and silk cocoons. Farmers had to count, separately, their horses, mules, and donkeys. The census for manufactures was equally detailed.

Starting in 1820, Congress also began expanding the list of census questions about the people themselves (what the Census Bureau calls population questions). In the 1840 Census Act, Congress called for the collection of information about "the pursuits, industry, education, and resources of the country." Pure curiosity combined with a growing awareness of America as a highly successful nation inspired the expansion of the census. Only 37 years earlier, people identified themselves by the state of their birth, as a "Virginian," for example, or a "Georgian." Americans' sense of nationhood, however, had grown quickly. With this national consciousness came an interest in knowing just who the Americans were.

In every census the list of population questions grew longer. By 1850, the population questions included ones like: What do you do for a living? What is the value of any *real estate* you own? Do you receive a war pension? What was your place of birth? Are you able to read and write? How much schooling have you had? Are any of your family members deaf and dumb, blind, insane, *paupers* (people

Expansion of Census

The census kept growing during the rest of the 19th century. By 1890, the census asked over 13,000 questions! Only a small number of the questions were asked of the general population, but there were over 200 separate questionnaires for special topics.

so poor they had to rely on public charity), or convicts? The census also asked questions about people's wages and taxes paid, newspapers, religion, schools, libraries, and more. As a result, the report of the 1850 census data was more than 2,000 pages long—somewhat longer than the 56-page report of the 1790 census!

After each census, newspapers published articles about the increases in the nation's population, its *literacy*, and its wealth. People marveled at the growth since the last census and wondered what the next census would reveal. By 1850, Americans were immensely proud of the progress their country had made so quickly. They liked what they saw when they gazed into the mirror of the census and they wanted to know more.

To some Americans, their country's spectacular growth in this period was proof of the superiority of its political system: democracy. To others, the country's success seemed a mark of God's favor. Many Americans came to feel that it was America's *manifest destiny* (manifest means "obvious") to cover the continent from the Atlantic to the Pacific and as far north and south as it could go. James Benner, editor of *The New York Herald* newspaper, summed up the feelings of Americans at this time when he wrote in 1846: "A people of twenty millions, spread over a continent of immense surface, a wonder to ourselves and a wonder to the world!"

There was one aspect of their country, however, that not all Americans were pleased with: slavery. It was soon to cause a major split in the nation's unity.

5

Before the Civil War
The Census Predicts Disaster

The 1850 census revealed that nearly 4 million of the 12 million people in the South—one-third of the total Southern population—were enslaved. About 75 percent of the slaves worked on huge cotton plantations. At the time only 20 percent of the nation's industry and one-third of its railroad system were located in the South.

In the Northern states in 1850, there were 19 million people. In most states north of the Mason-Dixon line, slavery had been declared illegal and there were few slaves. In Delaware, Maryland, Kentucky, and Missouri, the states that bordered the South and permitted slavery yet joined the Northern side in the Civil War, there were fewer than 400,000 slaves. Eighty percent of the nation's industry was located in the North, and railroads linked farms, factories, and ports. Most of the Northern farms were small and were worked primarily by family members.

The North's population was growing much faster than the South's. Of every nine immigrants arriving in America between 1810 and 1860, eight landed at ports in the North such as New York, Boston, Philadelphia, and Baltimore. The great majority of these immigrants stayed in Northern states and territories where the land was cheaper and suited to productive small-scale farming and opportunities in manufacturing, mines, and industry were plentiful.

Cotton, Crisis, and Compromise

The Northern and Southern states were split by growing differences in population and economy. They were also split by slavery. Northerners and Southerners had disagreed about slavery in America since the first days of independence. If Americans held that "all men are created equal," as it said in the Declaration of Independence, some wondered, how could they allow slavery to exist? This contradiction had long troubled many Northerners, including Puritans, Quakers, and members of other religious groups. In 1820, when Missouri applied to become a state, the contradiction became a crisis.

At the root of the crisis was cotton. Cotton had become the biggest money-making crop of the South. But because cotton plants took nutrients out of the soil, wearing it out after a few years, cotton farmers (called *planters*) had to plant new fields constantly. New land was essential to successfully growing cotton. Planters needed the new land in the western territories—like Missouri—to continue their cotton plantation system.

Slaves, planters believed, were also essential to cotton plantations. Planting, tending, and picking cotton were hot, backbreaking chores. Even with unpaid slave labor, cotton plantations were often not profitable. Southern politicians—who were usually also

There were many Southerners, including Virginia-born Presidents Washington and Jefferson, who believed that slavery was an evil. George Washington wrote in 1786 "…there is no man living who wishes more sincerely than I do to see some plan adopted for [slavery's] abolition." Jefferson wrote that he hoped the prohibition against importing slaves in 1808 "would stop the increase of this great political and moral evil…"Despite their understanding of the evils of slavery, both men owned many slaves. They compromised their moral principles because they believed their farms could not function without slave labor.

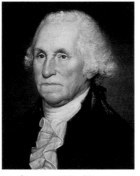

George Washington

Thomas Jefferson

planters—insisted that slavery be permitted in the new western territories.

Northerners, on the other hand, believed it was important that slavery not be allowed in the territories. Some Northerners believed slavery was unethical and opposed allowing slavery in the territories on moral grounds. Many Northern farmers and craftsmen wanted the territories to prohibit slavery for more practical reasons. How would a free farmer who had to pay his laborers be able to compete with a farmer who used unpaid slave labor? To whom would a cobbler sell his shoes if enslaved craftsmen at the nearby plantations provided the plantation owners and slaves with shoes at no cost?

So, when Missouri, whose state constitution permitted slavery, applied to join the Union (a popular term for the United States), Northerners were bitterly opposed. It was not only the question of slavery that mattered. Missouri would, like all other states, send two senators to Congress. There had been an equal number of slave state and free state senators, and Missouri would upset the balance. The new Missouri senators would vote with the other *slave states* (states permitting slavery) on the many issues about which North and South disagreed.

In 1820, congressmen worked out a deal, known as the Missouri Compromise. Missouri would enter the Union as a slave state, and Maine would enter as a free state, keeping the balance between free and slave states in the Senate. Congress also compromised on where slavery could be permitted in the territories. Slavery would be allowed in territory south of a line drawn along the southern border of Missouri west to California. Territory north of the line would be free.

The Debates of 1850

During the next 30 years, eight more states applied for admission to the Union. Congress made sure that every free state admitted was balanced by a slave state. Missouri, Arkansas, Florida, and Texas were balanced by Maine, Michigan, Iowa, and Wisconsin. Then, in

1850, California applied as a free state—despite the fact that most of its territory was below the 1820 Missouri Compromise line. The debate in Congress was even angrier about California than it had been about Missouri.

By 1850, slavery had become a very emotional question in America. The voices of *abolitionists* (people who wanted to outlaw slavery) in the North had grown loud. Southern politicians felt their way of life was threatened and defended slavery. They justified slavery on the grounds that the Africans and their descendants were less than the equal of whites. Slaves, they said, needed to be "protected" by wiser and kind owners. "Slavery," Senator John

Counting African Americans

Historians have only scattered and incomplete information about the black population before 1790. The records of companies that were in the business of importing slaves, like the English Royal African Company, provide some useful information. Not all sales of slaves, however, went through established businesses. Slave importers had to pay a tax (called a duty) on their imports, so they often smuggled slaves illegally into the colonies. Smugglers left no records.

Some colonial governments took thorough censuses of their white and black populations, but other colonies never held a census at all. Churches in the colonial period often recorded births, christenings, marriages, and deaths, but generally only for whites. The colony of South Carolina passed a law in 1704, for example, that required churches to register these important events, but blacks and Indians were specifically excluded.

The first census in 1790 revealed that out of a population of nearly four million, more than 757,000 people were of African descent. Nine out of ten African Americans were enslaved and nine out of ten slaves lived in Virginia, South Carolina, Maryland, North Carolina, and Georgia. On the eve of the Civil War, although the African American population had grown to four million, still only 10 percent were free.

Most historians believe that the censuses before the Civil War did not fully count the African Americans because slave owners, or their white managers (called *overseers*) did not make complete reports. In some states, slaves counted as taxable property, so owners had a good reason for not counting everyone. Old people and infants especially were under-reported.

Calhoun of South Carolina said, was "a positive good." Senator Brown of Mississippi claimed it was "a blessing for the slave."

In 1850, in the midst of the debate in Congress about California, a new debate opened. Congress had to vote on changes proposed for the 1850 census. Northern congressmen supported, among other changes, more questions about the slaves. Instead of asking the head of the household to simply provide a count of his slaves, now the census would ask for each slave's name, age, place of birth, number of children living and dead, and other details.

These questions outraged Southern congressmen who feared what the questions might reveal. Information, for example, about

The end of slavery did not end the undercount of African Americans. The Census Bureau acknowledges that even in the 20th century the census has missed more African Americans than any other racial or *ethnic* group. In Chapter 10 we'll look at why the Census Bureau still undercounts African Americans and other ethnic minorities.

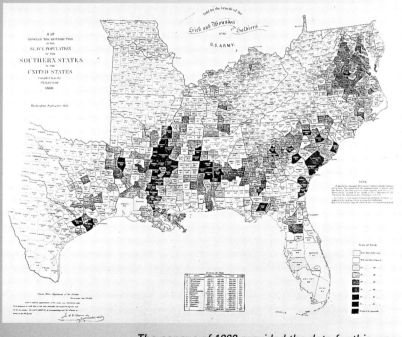

The census of 1860 provided the data for this map.

slaves' birthplaces, might show how many slaves had been sold away from their homes and families. If slaves' children did not survive at the rate that white children did (as they did not), people would conclude that slavery was not "a positive good" or a "blessing." Senator King of Alabama accused Northern senators of suggesting the new questions to stir a "fanatical spirit" of abolition that could split the Union.

In 1850, Congress made new political compromises. California entered the Union as a free state. In exchange, Northern congressmen agreed to pass a new and much tougher Fugitive Slave Act, which was designed to force Northerners to return runaway slaves. As for the 1850 census bill, as a part of the spirit of compromise, the questions about slaves were limited. Although the 1850 census, for the first time, noted every free individual's name and responses (rather than just totaling all the family members under the head of the household's name), Congress agreed this would not apply to slaves. The names of slaves were not listed; each slave was identified only by a number.

The End of Compromise

The political compromises did not last long. Many events in the 1850s led the North and South to war in 1861. Harriet Beecher Stowe wrote a novel called *Uncle Tom's Cabin,* a heart-wrenching story of a slave girl running from a vicious slave dealer. The book sold two million copies in America by 1861 and made Northerners more aware of the human tragedy of slavery. A civil war broke out in Kansas in 1856 over whether that state would be a free or slave state, and hundreds of people died. When the Supreme Court ruled in 1857 that slaves were property even when taken to free states, some Northerners saw that Southern slavery made their own states less free.

But, ultimately, the doom of the United States as a half-free and half-slave country was in the population numbers. In 1810, there had been an equal number of senators from free and slave states

135,000 SETS, 270,000 VOLUMES SOLD.

UNCLE TOM'S CABIN

FOR SALE HERE.

AN EDITION FOR THE MILLION, COMPLETE IN 1 Vol., PRICE 37 1-2 CENTS.
"   "   IN GERMAN, IN 1 Vol., PRICE 50 CENTS.
"   .   "   IN 2 Vols., CLOTH, 6 PLATES, PRICE $1.50.
SUPERB ILLUSTRATED EDITION, IN 1 Vol., WITH 153 ENGRAVINGS.
PRICES FROM $2.50 TO $5.00.

The Greatest Book of the Age.

Many Northerners were indifferent to the condition of slaves in the South until Uncle Tom's Cabin *helped them imagine one girl's grief and suffering. Stage versions of the book toured the Northern and Western states, moving audiences to tears.*

and a nearly equal number of representatives. But by 1850, there were more free state senators than slave state senators. In the House of Representatives, free state congressmen outnumbered slave state congressmen by 147 to 90.

The slave states knew they were destined to become an ever smaller minority in the Union. Southerners saw the day fast approaching when the North would impose its views on slavery. In 1858, before he was elected president, Abraham Lincoln declared:

"A House divided against itself cannot stand. I believe this government cannot endure permanently half slave and half free. I do not expect the Union to be dissolved—I do not expect the house to fall—but I do expect it will cease to be divided. It will become all one thing, or all the other."

As soon as Lincoln won election as president, South Carolina left the Union. It was followed by ten other states from Virginia to Texas. The Civil War was about to start.

Lincoln's *emancipation* (freeing) of the slaves in the Southern states in 1863 and the South's surrender in 1865 ended America's debate about slavery. The country, however, would shortly face difficult, new questions about race and nationality.

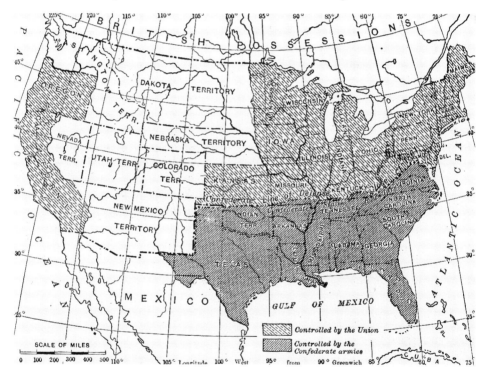

This map shows the division in 1861 between the northern states that remained in the U.S. and the southern states which had seceded from the U.S.

6

From the Golden Door to the Closed Door

Immigration 1870–1920

The North and South fought for four years from 1861 to 1865. When the war ended, the flow of immigrants from Europe—which had continued even during the war—became a flood. Over 2.5 million people arrived in the 1870s, and over 5 million arrived in the 1880s. In the two decades after the war, most of the immigrants were from Germany, Ireland, Norway, Denmark, and Sweden.

Today, there are many more people who would like to move to America than our laws will allow to come. But, in the 20 years after the Civil War, America needed more immigrants. Railroad companies needed workers to build railroads, coal mining companies needed miners, and factories needed both craftsmen and unskilled labor. Western states needed people to settle their empty lands and

Before they were allowed to stay in the United States, newly arriving immigrants at Ellis Island were inspected for any health problems by government officers.

develop their economies. Many businesses and states even sent representatives to Europe to attract people to America by advertising opportunities for jobs and a better life in this country.

It was not difficult to attract immigrants from Ireland and Germany in mid-century. The Irish depended on their potato crop for food, but starting in 1845 the potatoes were nearly completely destroyed in the ground by disease. People in Ireland were starving to death, and many Irish left for America. In fact, in the 15 years before the Civil War, 25 percent of the entire population of Ireland had come to America! After the war, the Irish continued to arrive.

In Germany in 1848, many people joined in a revolution against the German government for more political freedom. When the government won the struggle, however, many people fled for their lives. Between 1850 and 1860 nearly a million Germans came to America.

At the time many Americans welcomed the immigrants, not only for economic reasons, but because they believed America had a mission to encourage human liberty. They believed the American Revolution was about freedom from British oppression. In the same spirit, Americans wanted to provide a refuge for others seeking freedom and opportunities not available in the Old World. In 1883, a Jewish *immigrant*, Emma Lazarus, wrote a poem for the Statue of Liberty that expressed this ideal:

> Give me your tired, your poor,
> Your huddled masses yearning to breathe free,
> The wretched refuse of your teeming shore,
> Send these, the homeless, tempest-tost to me,
> I lift my lamp beside the golden door!

The golden door was the entrance to America. Between the end of the Civil War and 1890 nearly ten million European immigrants walked through it.

The statue with her lamp of liberty represents America.

40

America Changes Its Mind

After the Civil War ended, more and more American workers found jobs in the new factories that were producing all kinds of goods from textiles to gunpowder. The growth of industry in America after the war was spectacular and meant job opportunities for many. Working conditions in the factories, however, were often miserable. Men, women, and even children often found themselves working more than ten hours a day at noisy, dangerous machines for low wages. Workers began to form or join *labor unions* (labor unions are organized groups of workers in the same type of industry) in increasing numbers as a way to increase their wages or improve their working conditions. Sometimes workers in a union went on strike, which means they refused to work in an effort to force their employers to agree to their demands.

In 1886, more than 600,000 people were out of work due to strikes and to factory closings caused by strikes. In May, at an otherwise peaceful meeting of some strikers at Haymarket Square in Chicago, a bomb suddenly exploded. Seven policeman and four civilians died in the bombing or in the police gunfire just afterward. Although the Chicago police never discovered who threw the bomb, foreigners were blamed. Six German immigrants (and one native-born American) were sentenced to death. Another German was sentenced to a long prison term.

This was the first of a series of ugly anti-foreign incidents that occurred over the next 30 years. These actions reflected a change of opinion in America about immigrants. Here are some of the opinions Americans voiced about incoming immigrants in the 1880s and 1890s:

"These people are not Americans, but the very scum and offal [rubbish] of Europe.";

"…long-haired, wild-eyed, bad-smelling, atheistic [not believing in God], reckless foreign wretches…."; and

"…beaten men from beaten races."

About 300,000 Chinese came to California from the 1850s through the 1870s to work in mining or building railroads. Because the Chinese were so poor, they were willing to work in America for very low wages. When economic depression hit, white workers became angry at the Chinese for competing against them for jobs. In 1882, Congress passed the Chinese Exclusion Act that ended Chinese immigration.

Some Americans wanted to close the golden door. As one observer said, "the old cry in favor of unrestricted immigration has almost entirely ceased." What had changed their minds?

Some Americans feared that immigrants were bringing radical political ideas to America. Some of the strikers who people read about or saw were *socialists*, who wanted the government to take over businesses, and *anarchists*, who wanted no government at all. Those ideas scared Americans, especially when the people voicing the ideas were the same people leading strikes that ended in violence.

In addition, by the end of the century, there was no longer boundless open land left in the country. Much of the good land was already claimed. People feared that immigrants were taking land that was becoming scarce.

New immigrants often took the exhausting, difficult, and dangerous jobs in mining and in factories. Native-born Americans who were fluent in English usually didn't want this work, since they had better job possibilities. When there was an economic depression, though (which happened frequently in the 1880s, 1890s, and early 1900s), and work became hard to find, they changed their minds. Then, it looked as if foreigners were taking opportunities from them.

Religious prejudice had a lot to do with closing the door to immigration. After 1890, more and more immigrants came from Italy and

Discrimination *against foreigners was often expressed not just in words, but in actions. In 1880, in Denver, Colorado, a mob attacked people in a Chinese neighborhood, but were turned back by firemen using hoses (shown above). In New Orleans in 1891, eleven Italians were lynched (that means killed by a mob). In Hazelton, Pennsylvania, in 1897, striking Polish- and Hungarian-born mine workers were attacked by a sheriff's posse as they walked, unarmed, to a nearby town. Twenty-one were killed. In 1920 in southern Illinois, after two Italians were accused of a kidnapping, mobs attacked immigrant neighborhoods and burned people's homes.*

central and eastern Europe. Most of the Italian, as well as the Irish immigrants, were Catholic. Many Americans had English and northern European Protestant ancestors. In Europe, Protestants and Catholics had a long history of bitter feelings. Some Americans feared the Catholic Church and the pope were against liberty and individual freedom, they imagined Catholic plots to take over America.

Many Jews from Russia also came to America. In the same way that people believed Catholics were following the pope's orders, people believed Jews were acting on orders of an international Jewish conspiracy. Many jobs, clubs, and colleges refused to admit Jews.

Other prejudices worked against the new immigrants. People from Russia, Poland, Italy, Hungary, and other countries had different customs and wore different clothing. Some of them had darker skin than immigrants from England, Scotland, and Ireland, and they didn't speak English. They seemed quite different from the earlier immigrants.

43

Finally, many of these new immigrants had fled Europe with little other than the clothes they wore. They could not afford to buy land and had to settle in big cities in overcrowded housing. Poverty and crowding led to disease and crime in the cities. Many Americans, however, didn't understand this and believed that the immigrants were criminal and dirty by nature. In fact, many immigrants were from the countryside of Europe and were also shocked at the conditions in big American cities.

Closing the Door

The strength of anti-foreign feelings rose and fell in the decades after 1880, but the feelings never went away. Over time, Congress considered various ways to limit immigration. In 1882, it passed a law excluding new immigrants from China. In 1917, it passed a literacy test for immigrants that would exclude those who could not read and write. In 1918, Congress voted to allow the government to *deport* (send back home) foreigners who belonged to certain *radical* political organizations.

In 1921, Congress put in place strict numerical limits (called *quotas*) on new immigration. The quota for each nation was equal to 3 percent of the number of that nation's immigrants counted in the 1910 census. Only 350,000 new immigrants were allowed to enter in 1922—a sharp reduction from the 805,000 who entered in 1921. The law discriminated against people from southern and eastern Europe because they had smaller total numbers in the 1910 census than people from England, Ireland, and northern Europe.

Then, in 1924, Congress changed the 1921 immigration law so that the 1890 census (rather than the 1910 census) became the basis for the quotas. The law reduced the total quota for immigrants to 165,000. The quotas for central and eastern European immigrants became even smaller. The number of Italian immigrants permitted to enter, for example, fell from 42,000 to 4,000, the Polish quota fell from 31,000 to 6,000, and the Greek quota fell from 3,000 to 100!

44

The 1920 Census

Twenty-six million immigrants landed in America in the 50 years after the Civil War. Many of them, especially after 1880, settled in cities. Not only were the big cities expanding with immigrants, but the rate at which women were having babies in rural areas was falling. The 1920 census revealed that, for the first time, a majority of Americans lived in towns or cities.

The 1920 census should have resulted in more congressmen for states that had big cities. States that had a largely rural population should have lost representation. Political power should have shifted in favor of people living in urban areas.

But Congress refused to reapportion itself based on the 1920 census results, even though the Constitution requires it! Rural congressmen did not want to lose their seats in Congress, and they did not want power to go to the immigrant-filled cities. Congress did not reapportion itself until 1929. Even then, as we will see in Chapter 9, political power remained in the hands of rural representatives. Not until the 1960s would this unfairness be dealt with.

7

The Great Depression

A New Role for the Census

Americans stopped worrying about immigration after 1929 because few Europeans wanted to come. Europeans had no reason to uproot themselves. There were few jobs to be had in America and wages were falling. In the 1930s America was in the midst of what became known as the Great Depression.

There had been many economic depressions in the country's history. These depressions usually lasted a few years and then prosperity returned. The Great Depression was different. Never had a depression been so severe or lasted so long. It started in 1929 and finally lifted as America entered World War II in 1941.

The Great Depression began with "The Crash" in October 1929. What crashed? The price of stocks. Stocks are pieces of companies (called *shares*) that people can buy and sell. Shares of stocks represent ownership of a company. The price of a company's stock goes up or down depending on the value of the company. The price also depends on demand—how many people want to buy the stock. (When more people want to buy a stock than sell it, the price goes up. When there are more sellers

Depression Defined

What is a depression? During an economic depression, general economic activity slows down. People buy fewer goods, factories produce fewer goods, prices sometimes fall, and there is more unemployment.

Many people had bought stocks "on margin." This meant they only paid a portion of the stock's price—sometimes as little as 10 percent—and borrowed the rest. People assumed the price of their stock would go up. They counted on selling the stock in the future at a much higher price to pay back the rest of the original cost. When stock prices suddenly plummeted, people had to pay back the amount they owed right away... even if it meant selling the car and house to get the cash to do so.

than buyers, the price goes down.) Since 1924, the average price of stocks had been rising. Then, in 1927, nearly everyone, including many average people who didn't have a lot of money to spare, began to buy stocks like mad, pushing the prices up further. Suddenly, on October 24, 1929, everyone panicked and wanted to sell their stocks. No one wanted to buy. Prices of stocks fell dramatically. The market for stocks (the *stock market*) crashed.

By mid-November, the average price of a stock had fallen 40 percent. This meant that an average share of stock that someone had bought for $100 was now worth only $60. Many stocks fell even more: A share of RCA (Radio Corporation of America) that sold for

$505 in mid-September was only worth $28 in mid-November. Many people had borrowed money from their stock brokers to buy their stocks and now had to pay back those loans. Banks were in trouble, too. People wanted to take their cash savings (called *deposits*) out of the banks. Unfortunately, the banks' owners had

The Great Depression and Farmers

For farmers, the Great Depression was devastating. Low prices for crops meant that farmers couldn't pay back debts. Then, creditors (often a bank that had loaned the farmer money to buy land or seeds) forced the farmer to sell his farm to pay off the overdue loans. Some farmers fought to keep their farms.

Time magazine reported this scene of a farm sale in 1933:

"A crowd of neighbors went over to John Hansel's place near Doylestown, Pennsylvania, to attend a sheriff's sale. A deputy first asked for bids on a five-year-old plow horse. Somebody bid 5 cents. Nobody raised it. Next a Holstein bull was put up. It was not worth more than 5 cents to anybody. Tough-muscled farm boys circulated in the crowd to make sure that no outsider thought three hogs worth more than 5 cents, or two calves worth more than 4 cents. Farmer Hansel's entire property brought $1.18. Nobody took anything away. Instead neighbors collected $25 for him and his three motherless children."

This photo was taken by Walker Evans who, with writer James Agee, produced a book called *Let Us Now Praise Famous Men*. The book revealed the poverty of rural, southern America, as well as the courage of the farmers. Evans and Agee were working for the WPA at the time.

loaned their deposits to the stockbrokers or used them to buy stocks! Within the next two years, thousands of banks closed and many people lost their savings.

Factories began to close and businesses failed because they didn't have enough buyers for their goods and services. People had no money to buy them. Millions of workers lost their jobs. By 1934, almost 27 percent of Americans were unemployed.

At about the same time, prices for farm products, like wheat and milk, were falling. Farmers who had borrowed money to buy seeds, fertilizer, and farm machines, as farmers often do, were in trouble, too. When farm prices fell, farmers couldn't earn enough money from selling their products to repay their loans. Because farmers had promised their farms to the banks as repayment in the event they didn't pay back their loans, many farmers were losing their farms.

Herbert Hoover was president in 1929 when the Great Depression started. At first he, like most other people, thought the economy would recover on its own as it had many times before. But President Hoover changed his mind quickly. He started government programs that spent billions of dollars to get the economy going again. Most of that money, however, was loaned to banks, railroads, and insurance companies, so that they would be able to operate and provide loans and jobs. Hoover did not believe that the federal government should help needy, unemployed people directly.

Franklin D. Roosevelt won the 1932 election over Herbert Hoover by a landslide. Many people blamed Hoover for the Great Depression, although it had many causes. Roosevelt actually continued many of the new programs Hoover started, but he also supported programs that provided jobs and direct aid. The two presidents had different personalities. Hoover was a rather gloomy person. FDR, although he had been crippled by a disease called polio, was a popular, optimistic, enthusiastic leader.

Herbert
Hoover

Franklin D.
Roosevelt

When Franklin Delano Roosevelt, who was often referred to by his initials, FDR, was elected president in 1932, he announced his "New Deal" for fighting the Great Depression. He proposed new laws to regulate banking and the stock market. He also created many new government agencies that provided jobs for the unemployed. The Civilian Conservation Corps (CCC) gave over two million men jobs planting new forests and improving the countryside. The Civil Works Administration (CWA) and then the Works Progress Administration (WPA) eventually employed over ten million Americans in building schools, highways, sewer systems, and airports. The WPA also gave jobs to unemployed writers, musicians, and artists.

The Census and the Depression

Despite the CCC, CWA, and WPA, millions of people were still unemployed in the mid-1930s. But how many millions? No one knew for sure because the census of 1930 was taken just as the Great Depression began.

Some congressmen called for an extra census in 1935 that would provide better numbers about the unemployed. President Roosevelt was not in favor of it, however. Although the New Deal was in operation, the country was still in a deep depression. He was not eager to have numbers that would show his administration had not yet solved the country's unemployment problem.

The call for better, more detailed information about unemployment, however, did not go away. In fact, senators and congressmen needed those numbers even more because a new federal agency, the Federal Emergency Relief Administration, was sending federal relief money for needy people (called *grants-in-aid*) to their states. The states had to figure out how best to distribute money to their citizens. By 1936, these grants-in-aid were $2 billion and one-third of the entire *federal budget*.

The Social Security Act of 1935 also created demand for more detailed information about the population. The Social Security Act was passed by Congress to provide federal money for public health, the elderly, poor families with children, and unemployment insurance. Data from the census were to be used to divide up the money among states.

The New Deal programs and the Social Security Act reflected a new vision of the role of government. People were beginning to believe that government should make sure that all Americans achieved a certain minimum *standard of living*. The federal government took on the responsibility of seeing that everyone had basic educational opportunities, decent housing, and could meet minimum health standards. Without more information about the population, it was hard to know whom to help and how much help was needed.

People in cities who worked in factories were also desperate. Child labor laws had not yet been passed. Poor children worked to make money to help their families survive. Time *magazine reported on March 13, 1933, that "Girls were sleeping in subways because they could not afford the price of a bed. Hospitals were filling with women who had worked themselves into a state of collapse for a pittance." At the time, a hatmaker who made two dozen hand-knit hats in a week was paid a total of 80 cents. An "apron girl" earned 2 1/2 cents for each apron she sewed. She earned 20 cents a day.*

The Great Depression changed census-taking in America. If the government was going to be more active in helping its citizens, it had to ask more questions. By 1940, it was clear that many new questions would have to be added to the census to gather all the information needed by the new programs. In 1935, for example, the Rural Electrification Authority was started to bring electricity to the 90 percent of farms that did not have it. So, the 1940 census asked questions about the heating and lighting in people's houses. Poor housing was also a problem, so the census asked the value of people's houses and whether their houses had indoor plumbing. Enumerators were told to report whether a house they visited needed major repairs. The government wanted to know the extent of the problems in order to help fix them.

Although the New Deal programs helped the economy recover, unemployment was still high in 1940. In 1940, 15 percent of Americans were still unemployed, compared with less than 5 percent in 1999. America's entry into World War II in 1941 ended the Great Depression in America because the government needed so many goods— from airplanes to uniforms to tents—to fight World War II. Many found jobs in new war-related factories. Also, many people were "employed" by the military services.

The government also had to ask questions more often. Starting in 1940, the government began to count the unemployed every month. This way, the government would be able to take some steps before unemployment reached a crisis level. The monthly unemployment count, which used a sample (more about that in Chapter 9) of people to stand for the whole country, became known as the Current Population Survey.

After 1940, the Census Bureau expanded on the idea of more frequent counts using samples (which are called *surveys*). Today, the Census Bureau conducts over 100 surveys. The Census Bureau collects information on household spending, which helps predict whether the economy is headed for a depression and whether prices are generally rising or falling. The Census Bureau also asks people questions about their recent direct experience with crime. This survey helps law enforcement agencies prepare to combat crimes and help victims. Another survey, which is taken weekly, asks people what kind of illnesses they have had recently. This survey helps health agencies see which diseases are spreading and where.

Information Overload

The Census Bureau couldn't produce the final census results of 1880 until 1887—just three years before the next census was to start! In the 1880s the U.S. population was 50 million. By 1940, the U.S. population was more than two and a half times larger: 132 million. You might imagine that counting the population of 1940 would take two and a half times longer than it did in 1880. If it had, that would have meant the 1940 census results would be released in 1957, seven years after the next census would be taken. Fortunately, two things helped the U.S. census keep to its decennial schedule: better *technology* and *sampling*.

8

Counting Millions
Punched Cards, Computers, and Redheads

In 1880, it took seven years to count all the answers to census questions and put the information into reports. Why was it taking so long? For one thing, there were so many more people to count. In less than a century, the country's population had grown from 3.9 million to 50 million. And, the number of questions had grown tremendously. The 1790 census asked six questions; the 1880 census asked over 13,000 questions in 200 different lists.

The Census Bureau spent a lot of time cross-tabulating answers to the census questions, that is comparing the answers to one question with the answers to other questions to get new information and insights. For example, the census in 1880 gathered information on immigrants' country of birth, *illiteracy* (the inability to read), and age. It was possible, therefore, for the Census Bureau to cross-tabulate this information and figure out how many immigrants, by country of birth and by age, couldn't read.

The process involved using a large "tally sheet" that had lots of rows (in this example, for all possible countries of birth) and columns (for every age). Census Bureau clerks would look at every questionnaire and make a mark in the appropriate box for every illiterate person. You can see why doing this for millions of census forms would take years!

Punched Card Automation

Fortunately for the census, a young engineer named John Hollerith came to work for the Census Bureau in 1881. Hollerith saw how much effort it took the clerks to tally the census. He could see that an electrical machine could do much of the clerks' work and do it faster.

Hollerith found that he could punch holes in a card so that the location of each hole represented a *characteristic* of (something about) that person. For example, a hole in the top left corner would mean "male,"

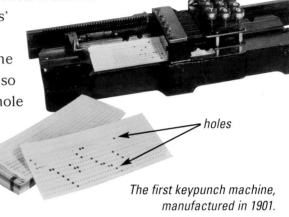

holes

The first keypunch machine, manufactured in 1901.

but a hole just to the right of it would mean "female." The next ten spaces on the card might represent ethnic background. A card with a hole in the first space and a hole in the ninth space might represent a male Italian-born American. For every American, there was one punched card. That meant for the 1890 census, Census Bureau employees punched almost 63 million cards.

Hollerith invented a machine that would count the holes on each card. The machine pushed a grid of 288 metal pins against the card. If a pin hit a hole, it would go through

John Hollerith formed a company to produce his tabulating machines. That company eventually became a part of International Business Machines—IBM.

The machines put a new kind of stress on office workers. Sometimes the clerical workers would use an eyedropper to siphon out the mercury from the little cups in the tabulating machine... so the machine wouldn't work and they could get a break from its tireless pace!

the hole and dip into a little cup of liquid metal called mercury, completing an electrical circuit. The electrical current moved the hand on a dial ahead one number. The machine, called a tabulating machine, could count all the holes in a card at one time.

It still took a lot of time for a clerk to punch the holes into the cards. But when it came time to count the cards, the machine could do the work much faster than a person. One clerk could process at least 1000 cards an hour. Using Hollerith's new machines, the Census Bureau finished the 1890 census in only two and a half years—a remarkable improvement over the seven years it took in 1880.

Electronic Computer Automation

Mechanical punch devices soon replaced hand-operated punches. In every decade, from 1890 to 1940, the tabulating machines that the Census Bureau used improved. By 1940, the Census Bureau could count 120,000 cards per hour.

Then, in 1946, technology at the Census Bureau took another leap forward. The Census Bureau spent $300,000 for the design of the world's first electronic computer for processing data. The computer would eventually be called UNIVAC (short for Universal Automatic Computer). When the Census Bureau purchased UNIVAC, it didn't actually exist, except in the minds of its two creators, John Presper Eckert and John W. Mauchly. It took Eckert and Mauchly five years and about $1 million to actually develop UNIVAC. They delivered the room-size machine to the Census Bureau in March 1951, in time to process some of the returns of the 1950 census.

UNIVAC was actually three connected machines. One part was a punched card reader that could transfer the information from the punched cards to magnetic tape. Another part was the printer. The most important part, though, was the Central Processing Unit (CPU). The CPU was made of 18,000 vacuum tubes.

Hollerith's tabulating machines processed information (gathered from punched cards) by counting the times a pin pushed through a card made contact with mercury. UNIVAC processed information

Vacuum tubes—glass tubes with the air removed—are no longer used in computers. Instead, today computers use transistors. Transistors are made of tiny pieces of a solid material called silicon, which can conduct an electrical current.

(gathered from magnetic tape) by counting electrical pulses as they passed through the vacuum tubes. Since electricity can pass through a vacuum much faster than a pin can make the journey through a punched card to a metal target, the new electronic computer was much faster than the mechanical tabulating machines.

Sampling

During the Great Depression of the 1930s, people realized that the government needed information about unemployment more often than once every ten years. But it clearly wasn't possible to ask everyone in the country their employment status every six months. Instead, the Census Bureau decided to sample the population every six months.

The word sample has a lot of meanings, but to statisticians—people who study statistics, a branch of mathematics that involves analyzing masses of numbers—sample has a very particular meaning. A *sample* is a "representative part" of a larger group. Using a sample, statisticians can draw conclusions about the entire population from which the sample was selected.

At first, you might think that sampling should be easy. But it's not. Imagine that someone wanted to use sampling to discover how many people in your school had black, brown, blond, and red hair. How many people would you have to sample to get a group that accurately reflects the school? If no redheads turned up in your sample, how sure would you be that there were no redheads at your school? And how would you pick the sample? Ask for volunteers? Pick four from each class? Which four? Statisticians can give you the answers to these questions.

In 1936, Literary Digest *magazine announced that Alf Landon would win the coming presidential election over Franklin D. Roosevelt (who is pictured here campaigning). The magazine's prediction was based on ballots sent out to readers. Of course, it turned out that Roosevelt won by a landslide. The magazine's readers were not a good sample of the American public .*

As mathematicians developed more information about statistics, the Census Bureau was able to use sampling to help cope with the problem of the ever-increasing size—and cost—of the census. In 1940 the decennial census used sampling for the first time. Only five percent of the population—every 20th person—was asked certain questions, such as veteran status and occupation.

Sampling is now a routine part of the census. In the 2000 census, everyone will be asked seven basic questions. But 17 percent of us will fill out the "long form" questionnaire that has an additional 46 questions. Statisticians can prove that the answers of the 17 percent will represent the answers of everyone.

9

The Census from 1930 to 1970
One Person, One Vote?

Remember that after the 1920 census, Congress didn't want to reapportion itself? Remember why not? The 1920 census revealed that more Americans lived in cities than in rural areas. Many of the people in those cities were immigrants from southern and eastern Europe. Many Americans had come to feel that the new immigrants threatened their jobs and their way of life. In Congress, representatives from rural areas did not want to see political power shift to cities filled with these immigrants.

Congress finally *did* pass a reapportionment bill in 1929 and reapportioned itself for the first time in nearly 20 years. Power, however, did not shift to the people in the cities. Even though there were fewer congressman from the more rural states, Congress continued to represent the people who lived on farms and in small towns to a greater extent than their numbers merited. In state legislatures, too, the growing numbers of city dwellers had fewer representatives than they deserved. How did that happen?

Voting Districts in the 19th Century

In the 1800s, (the early 1800s for the eastern states and later in the 1800s for the new western states) states began to subdivide their areas into counties. (Some states used other names for counties, like parishes in Louisiana, but it was the same idea.) The size of a county was generally no larger than the distance the farmer farthest away had to travel by wagon to the county seat (where the county government was) and back in a day. Counties were, therefore, about the same size and had about the same number of people. Each county, being equal in size and population, became a *state voting district* and sent one representative to the state legislature to make laws for the state.

States also divided their territory into larger, but roughly equal, areas for the purpose of electing representatives to Congress. These areas, called *congressional voting districts* or *congressional districts*, were also originally roughly equal in terms of population. Each congressional district elected one congressman. You can think of the state voting districts and congressional districts as identical maps, except, one has lots of squares (the state voting districts) and one has fewer squares (the congressional districts).

In the late 1800s, as the population of American cities grew, some of the squares began to have a lot more people than others. These were the state and congressional voting districts with large towns or cities within their borders. In many cases, the states should have shifted their districts' boundaries to equalize the population of districts. An 1842 federal law required that states make sure that congressional voting districts be equal in terms of population. States' constitutions generally required that the state legislature reapportion its membership following the decennial census. Nonetheless, wide differences among the populations of voting districts developed.

Voting Districts in the 20th Century

In some states, such as Tennessee, Illinois, and Alabama, legislators simply ignored the laws and stopped reapportioning about 1900. Other states passed laws that preserved political power for rural districts in the state legislature. Maryland, for example, specifically limited the number of representatives that Baltimore City would have. Some states failed to change outdated laws as common sense demanded. Vermont, for example, had a law that directed that every town would have one representative. In the early 1800s this made sense because all towns were about the same size. By 1963, however, it meant that a town of 38 people had one representative...as did Vermont's largest city of more than 35,000!

State legislatures also failed to adjust the boundaries of congressional voting districts to reflect the movement of people into cities. In one of the worst examples, New York's largest congressional district in 1930 had nearly 800,000 people while the smallest had 90,000—yet each district sent one congressman to Washington. The voice of one person in the smaller district was equal to the voices of nine people in the larger district.

Florida Misrepresentation

Florida had one of the most malapportioned legislatures by 1970. Over 50 percent of the seats in the Florida state legislature represented rural districts of north Florida, which contained less than 15 percent of the state's population.

Finally, in 1932, someone took the issue to court. The Supreme Court ruled that Congress deliberately did <u>not</u> require congressional districts to be equal in population when it passed the 1929 reapportionment bill. (When Congress finally passed a bill reapportioning itself in 1929, that law replaced the 1842 law. The 1929 law did not contain the old language about equality of districts.) *Malapportionment*, which means there are districts of very different population sizes, the Supreme Court said, was therefore acceptable! Then, in 1946, in a famous Supreme Court case called *Colegrove v. Green*, Justice Felix Frankfurter wrote that how states reapportioned their members was a political matter and not a matter of law for courts to decide.

The result was that by 1960 malapportionment among congressional districts was widespread. Fourteen of Michigan's 19 congressional districts, for example, were malapportioned. Twenty of Texas' 23 were, too. The largest district in Texas had 951,227

Inequality for African Americans

Because 75 percent of African Americans lived in cities by 1960, malapportionment meant that they were not fairly represented in state and national legislatures. The inequality in representation was part of the larger inequality blacks faced in life in America. In both the North and South, African Americans faced severe discrimination in finding housing and jobs.

Conditions were worse for African Americans in the South where unequal opportunities and conditions were established by law. Segregation laws (*segregation* literally means "separation") prevented black children from attending the better equipped and less crowded schools that most white children attended. Segregation laws also meant that blacks were not allowed in "white" restaurants, pools, parks, and other public places. Laws that required payment of *poll taxes* (taxes paid to vote) and kept mainly blacks from voting were widespread in the South.

Malapportionment, poll taxes, segregation, and discrimination prevented black Americans from exercising their *civil rights*, which means their rights as citizens. In December 1955, however, a courageous black woman in Alabama, named Rosa Parks, refused to give up her seat on a segregated bus to a white man. She was arrested, and the civil rights movement suddenly became one of

Rosa Parks seated on an Alabama bus.

Martin Luther King, Jr., (center) and his wife, Coretta,
march together with the March Against Fear.

the most publicized and important issues in America. In the late 1950s and through the 1960s, many Americans, black and white and from Northern and Southern states, worked to change these unfair laws.

The struggle for civil rights for black Americans was a hard one. After the Supreme Court ruled that all public schools had to be *integrated*, black children braved jeers and threats to go to formerly segregated schools throughout the South. People even died in the struggle for civil rights. In 1963, a black church was bombed in Birmingham, Alabama, and four girls were killed. In 1964, three college students who were encouraging African Americans to *register* to vote were killed by the Ku Klux Klan.

Dr. Martin Luther King, Jr., was the most famous civil rights leader of the 1960s. As a minister, he promoted peaceful protests against unjust laws and racial discrimination. Despite his nonviolent approach, Dr. King and many protesters, who marched with him in the South, were sometimes attacked by mobs and even local police. Dr. King's eloquence, his dignified approach, and his emphasis on the issues of equality and morality, however, made civil rights a cause for many Americans. Dr. King, who was assassinated in 1968, gave up his life for civil rights.

people while the smallest had only 216,371. The largest district in Georgia had 822,680 people while the smallest had 272,154. The Declaration of Independence said that "all men are created equal," but many people weren't equally represented in the U.S. Congress.

Changes of the 1960s

By 1960, about two-thirds of all white Americans and three-fourths of all African Americans lived in urban areas. In 1958, John F. Kennedy (who was a senator from Massachusetts at the time) summed up the problem:

"The apportionment of representation in our Legislatures and (to a lesser extent) in Congress has been either deliberately rigged or shamefully ignored so as to deny the cities and the voters that full and proportionate voice in government to which they are entitled."

The malapportionment meant unfair political representation, and also resulted in painfully unfair divisions of state and federal money. Certainly, representatives from rural areas were not as interested in urban issues or as eager to spend money on urban problems as representatives from those urban areas were.

The 1960s, however, was a time of change in the United States. It was the "civil rights era" when people were talking about, going to jail over, and even losing their lives over issues of fairness and equality. Between 1962 and 1964, the Supreme Court made historic rulings in a series of cases concerning voting districts at the state and congressional levels. The Court reversed direction and found that malapportioned voting districts *were* a matter of interest to the courts.

A number of Supreme Court cases led to the conclusion that state legislatures had to stick to the principle of "one man, one vote" in deciding how to draw state voting districts and congressional districts. ("One man, one vote" means all people's votes must count equally.) The Supreme Court said that the Constitution's fundamental goal was equal representation in the House of Representatives for equal numbers of people. This was, after all, the purpose of taking the census. The Supreme Court also pointed to the Fourteenth Amendment to the Constitution (ratified after the Civil War in 1868) that required that all Americans have "equal protection of the laws." The Court said that voting districts had to be "substantially equal" in population for people to be equally protected by the country's laws.

The "one man, one vote" principle meant that during the 1960s most of the states had to redraw their political maps and change their voting district lines. They used the 1960 census results to draw those maps—and some of those maps changed greatly. Now, after every decennial census, state legislatures meet to redraw the voting district lines with the goal of making each person's vote carry equal weight.

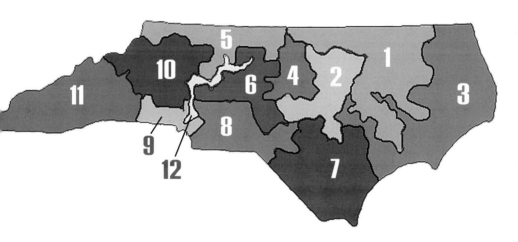

This is a map of the 12th district of North Carolina in 1997. It had the same number of people as the other North Carolina districts, but it is long, squiggly, and very narrow. Why did it have this odd shape? The Voting Rights Act of 1965 required states to create districts with majorities or substantial numbers of blacks, Hispanics, and other minority groups. Otherwise, it was feared—and was too often the case—that minorities would not have fair representation in Congress. Without the detailed, block-by-block information that the census provides, fair districting would not be possible. People still argue, however, whether such oddly-shaped districts as this one are the best way to achieve fair representation.

10

The 2000 Census

Focus on Accuracy

From the first census, people have wanted the census to do more than provide a simple count of the population. In 1790, the census asked each household how many men were more than 16 years old so Congress could know how many fighting age men it might draw on to defend the country. In the 1800s, the census expanded to satisfy Americans' curiosity about their rapidly growing nation and to demonstrate our country's strengths to the international community. During the Great Depression of the 1930s, the Census Bureau had to expand the census questionnaire. The Bureau had to ask questions about unemployment, for example, so that the federal government could decide how much money the WPA or the CCC, New Deal programs that provided jobs for the unemployed, should be granted.

In 1964, President Lyndon Johnson expanded on FDR's belief that the federal government had a responsibility to improve people's lives. He started "The War on Poverty." This was not a war against people fought with guns and bombs. It was a war to give people equal opportunities for education and jobs. It was fought with federal money and social programs. The laws that guided the programs often used data from the census to distribute money to those who deserved it.

Many of the programs started in the 1930s (like Social Security) and 1960s (like Medicare, Medicaid, and Headstart) are still operating

Sharing the Wealth

Lyndon Baines Johnson became president in 1963, following the assassination of President John F. Kennedy. America had enjoyed nearly two decades of prosperity after the end of World War II. President Johnson was aware, however, that the benefits of America's wealth were not evenly distributed among the peo-

Headstart volunteer and First Lady, Lady Bird Johnson, teaches a child in a Virginia school.

ple. His two major programs, the War on Poverty and the Great Society, included federal programs designed to share the nation's riches, include minorities in the political process, and improve everyone's quality of life.

The list of Johnson-era programs is long. One of the programs that was a part of The War on Poverty was called Headstart, a school program that tries to get poor children ready for kindergarten. President Johnson also proposed Medicare and Medicaid to help older people and poor people of any age to pay their medical bills. He initiated programs to improve housing, transportation, and parks, and to protect the environment. Many of his programs are still operating today.

today. Other programs have been added. Many of them continue to rely, entirely or in part, on census data to properly distribute funds. In 1998, about $170 billion in federal aid was given to the states and cities through programs that use census data to distribute the money. With billions of dollars at stake, as well as political power, it is very important that the census count everyone. But does it?

Getting an Accurate Count

The answer is no. In 1980, according to the U.S. General Accounting Office, the census missed 5.3 million people. In 1990, however, the *undercount* (inaccurately low count) meant that 9.7 million people were missed in the census. How did the Census Bureau miss so many people?

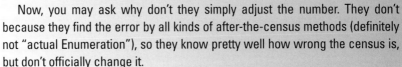

Adjusting the Undercount

The census failed to count 9.7 million people in 1990. However, it also counted 4.4 million people twice. So, the official, total number of people counted in the 1990 census–248.7 million–is actually only short by 5.3 million (9.7 million minus 4.4 million).

Now, you may ask why don't they simply adjust the number. They don't because they find the error by all kinds of after-the-census methods (definitely not "actual Enumeration"), so they know pretty well how wrong the census is, but don't officially change it.

One of the biggest problems for the Census Bureau is that some people do not fill out and mail back their questionnaires. In 1970, 78 percent of people filled and returned their questionnaires. In 1990, only 65 percent did. And in 2000, the Census Bureau predicts that only 61 percent will return their questionnaires by mail as they should. The Census Bureau follows up with personal visits, but the visits are expensive and too often people cannot be found or will not open their door.

Why aren't people responding to the census? There are a lot of different reasons. Some people just ignore the census questionnaire. It looks like one more piece of junk mail or just another *market survey*. Sometimes, in a house rented by college students, for example, no one takes responsibility for filling out the information. (Remember, census questionnaires are sent to household addresses, not to individual people.) Some people just don't understand how important the results are to our democratic government and to their economic well-being. And sometimes people are scared to answer the census questionnaire. They are afraid the government will use the information to harm them in some way.

Privacy

From 1790 until 1850, the census results were posted in two public places in each census district so that neighbors could come forward if they thought the information was incomplete or wrong.

Some Past Uses of Census Data

In the past, census data has been used in ways that would be illegal today, or that we would question. For example, during the Civil War, the Union Army used agricultural information collected by the census to identify farms where its troops marching through Georgia could find food. After the U.S. entered World War I (1914–1918), the Bureau searched its records to find men who were the right age to serve in the military. Unhappily, during World War II, when the U.S. was at war with Germany and its allies, including Japan, the Bureau identified where large numbers of Japanese Americans lived. This information helped government officials find citizens who were then forced to move into *internment camps* until the war ended September 2, 1945. In 1954, Congress thoroughly restricted the Bureau from releasing information about individuals. The restrictions are set out in Title 13 of the U.S. Code, which is the organized collection of federal laws.

People arrive at a Japanese internment camp in August 1942 during World War II.

Today, our ideas about privacy are different. According to the 1954 law that guides the operations of the Census Bureau today, the Bureau is absolutely prohibited from releasing information about individuals for 72 years after that information is gathered. People who violate the prohibition can be fined up to $5,000 and face as many as five years in jail.

Nonetheless, there are people who are afraid that the Census Bureau will give information about them to other U.S. government agencies. Illegal aliens worry that the Census Bureau will give their questionnaires to the Immigration and Naturalization Service, which might then be able to find and deport them. People who are in trouble with law enforcement or tax agencies often do not return their census questionnaires. Their fear is understandable, but it is not justified. The Census Bureau cannot and does not pass along any individual's information.

Counting Minorities

The biggest problem with the undercount is that it isn't evenly distributed across the country or throughout the population. More African Americans, Hispanics, and Native Americans are missed by the census than whites. In 1990, for example, the census missed

In 2000, for the first time, we will have more flexibility to identify our ethnic and racial backgrounds in the census. Instead of having to choose just one category (such as Caucasian, African American, Asian, or "other"), we can check as many ethnic or racial categories as we feel are appropriate. Tiger Woods, the young golf pro, for example, identifies himself as a "Cablasian," and might choose to check "Caucasian," "African American," and "Asian" on the 2000 census questionnaire.

1.3 percent of whites, but 5.7 percent of blacks and 5.0 percent of Hispanics were not counted. (There has been some improvement: 11.5 percent of African Americans were missed in 1950.) Because minorities tend to live in cities, the undercount has also meant that cities are shortchanged when it comes to political representation and federal and state funds.

Solutions for the Year 2000

What can be done about the undercount? The Census Bureau will spend over $100 million on public education before the 2000 census to let people know how important the census is and that they have nothing to fear from answering the questionnaire. The Bureau will also distribute questionnaires at public places like libraries and post offices. People who do not have an address at which to receive a questionnaire, or who are not otherwise included in the census, will have a way to participate. In addition, the Bureau is working with local religious and community leaders whom people know and trust in order to get the word out about the census.

Missing Urban Residents

Why are so many people in cities missed? There are lots of reasons. Here are some:

- Most of the nation's homeless live in cities and because they have no address, it is hard to get questionnaires to them.
- Cities are home to many recent immigrants. Some of those immigrants have come to the United States to escape oppression by the government of their former homeland. Some immigrants are suspicious of any government asking for personal information.
- Illegal immigrants often live in cities and fear (however unnecessarily) the Census Bureau.
- Young people, especially young men living in cities, tend to move frequently and sometimes are missed because they haven't established their own homes and are not clearly members of other households.

The Census Bureau would also like to use a kind of sampling called *nonresponse sampling* to make the census more accurate. With nonresponse sampling, the Bureau would try to reach at least 90 percent of the people in all census tracts. (A census tract is defined by the Census Bureau as a small geographic area where about 4,000 people live.) For those households who do not respond by mail or to enumerators' visits, however, the Bureau would use a sample of other households in the same tract to provide the missing data to get closer to a 100 percent count.

There is a great deal of argument about nonresponse sampling. The Bureau has long used sampling for many kinds of information. (The long form questionnaire is a sample, as are the Bureau's many surveys.) Using sampling, however, to make the basic count of people for the purpose of apportionment of congressional seats has not been done before. The language in the Constitution calls for an "actual Enumeration," and many people argue that using sampling is therefore unconstitutional. In January 1999, the Supreme Court issued a 5 to 4 decision against nonresponse sampling for the purpose of congressional apportionment. The ruling, however, does not prohibit nonresponse sampling for purposes of distributing federal funds or redrawing voting district boundaries. So, it is likely that the Census Bureau will issue two counts of the population— one using sampling and one not!

The debate about nonresponse sampling is not over. The Supreme Court ruling left open the possibility that Congress could change the laws that govern the census to allow nonresponse sampling. You will hear more about this question in years to come.

Beyond 2000

The cost of the census keeps going up. In 1970, it cost $250 million. In 1980, it cost over $1.1 billion. In 1990, the cost was over $2.5 billion. The Census Bureau has to think not only about counting everyone, but doing it more cheaply.

One way to reduce the cost of the census might be to eliminate

A Mirror of America: The 1990 Census

In 1790, the census revealed that there were about four million people in America. We know that most of these people were farmers, and that the majority of them (those who were not among the roughly 720,000 slaves of African ancestry) came from northern and western Europe. In 1990, the census revealed a very different picture of America. Here are a few facts about the American population two hundred years after the first census:

- Of a total population of 248.7 million, 75.2 percent lived in cities, 24.8 percent lived in the country, and less than .1 percent lived on farms.

- There were 115 million workers more than 16 years old in the United States. More than 73 percent drove alone to work, 13.4 percent carpooled, and only 5.3 percent used public transportation. The rest walked to work or worked at home.

- Almost 15 percent of families with related children less than 18 years old had incomes below the poverty line, which meant that 9.7 million families with kids lived in poverty.

- A total of 54,536 houses in America used solar power for heating.

- Seventy-five percent of the population more than 25 years old had high school diplomas and 20 percent had college degrees.

- Only 53.3 percent of people lived in the same house they did five years earlier. (People in West Virginia were most likely to stay put; 64.7 percent lived in the same house. On the other hand, only 34.7 percent of Nevadans lived in the same house.)

- Nearly 20 million people in America were foreign-born. There were about 1,536,000 immigrants in 1990: About 957,600 came from North and Central America, 318,600 came from Asia and the Middle East, 85,800 came from South America, 35,900 came from Africa, and 112,400 came from Europe.

- There were about 17,671,000 children between the ages of 10 and 14, but there were 431,000 more boys than girls. The average 12-year-old can expect to live another 64.3 years.

Remember how almost everyone in America in 1790 lived with a family? In 1990, over 1.1 million people lived in correctional institutions, 1.8 million lived in nursing homes, almost 2 million lived in college dormitories, 190,000 lived in homeless shelters, and about 50,000 lived on the streets.

the long form questionnaire. It might be replaced with monthly surveys that ask the same questions, but of fewer people. The information would also be more up-to-date than the decennial data.

Technology is already helping to cut the costs of the census. In 1990, all the completed questionnaires were still converted to punched cards before being tallied by computer. In 2000 the questionnaires will be read directly by computers. The Census Bureau is exploring using the telephone and Internet to ask questions and tally answers. It also expects to put most of its reports on the Internet and reduce printing costs.

You and the Census

When your family completes the 2000 census questionnaire, you will be participating in the U.S. census, the oldest continuing census in the world. You will be one more link in a long chain that stretches from 1790 to 2000 and into the future. The census questions and results have changed over the years, reflecting changes in America over time. The methods we have used to take the census have changed thoroughly, too. The census, however, has always been the means for distributing political power. Now it guides the distribution of economic power, too, in the form of billions of dollars in federal funds. Make sure you get counted!

You can learn more about the census and access data from past censuses by visiting the Census Bureau's website. www.census.gov

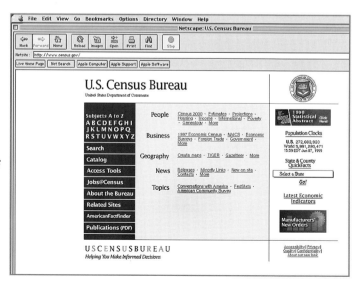

2000 Census Long Form Questions[1]

What is this person's name?

What is this person's telephone number?

What is this person's sex?

What is this person's age and date of birth?

Is this person Spanish/Hispanic/Latino?

What is this person's race? Mark one or more races.

What is this person's marital status?

Has this person attended regular school or college at any time in the last year? What grade level was this person attending?

What is the highest degree or level of school this person has completed?

What is this person's ancestry or ethnic origin?

Does this person speak a language other than English at home? What is this language? How well does this person speak English?

Where was this person born?

Is this person a citizen of the United States?

When did this person come to live in the United States?

Did this person live in this house 5 years ago? Where did this person live 5 years ago?

Does this person have any of the following long-lasting conditions? (list of disabilities follows)

Because of a physical, mental, or emotional condition lasting 6 months or more, does this person have any difficulty in doing any of the following activities? (learning, dressing, getting around, working, etc.)

Was this person under 15 years of age on April 1, 2000?

Does this person have any of his/her own grandchildren under the age of 18 living in this house or apartment? Is this grandparent currently responsible for most of the basic needs of any grandchildren under the age of 18 who live here? How long has this grandparent been responsible for the(se) grandchildren?

Has this person ever served on active duty in the U.S. Armed Forces, military Reserves, or National Guard? When did this person serve on active duty in the U.S. Armed Forces? In total, how many years of active-duty military service has this person had?

LAST WEEK, did this person do ANY work for pay or profit?

At what location did this person work LAST WEEK?

How did this person usually get to work LAST WEEK? If car, truck, or van was used, how many people, including this person, rode to work in the car, truck, or van LAST WEEK?

What time did this person usually leave home to go to work LAST WEEK? How many minutes did it usually take this person to get from home to work LAST WEEK?

LAST WEEK, was this person on layoff from a job? Had this person been looking for work during the last 4 weeks?

When did this person last work, even for a few days?

Industry or Employer: Describe clearly this person's chief job activity or business last week. What kind of business or industry was this?

Occupation: What kind of work was this person doing and what were this person's most important duties?

Was this person an employee of a profit or non-profit company, a government, or self-employed?

How many weeks did this person work last year? How many hours per week?

Income Last Year: Describe the type of income this person made last year (wages, interest and dividends, welfare payments, etc.).

What was this person's total income last year?

Is this house, apartment, or mobile home owned or rented?

Which best describes this building: a mobile home, detached house, building with apartments, boat or RV?

About when was the building first built?

When did this person move into this house, apartment, or mobile home?

How many rooms do you have?

How many bedrooms do you have?

Do you have complete plumbing facilities?

Do you have complete kitchen facilities?

Do you have telephone service?

Which fuel do you use for heat: gas, oil, kerosene, wood, solar energy?

How many vehicles do you have?

Is there a business on this property? How many acres is this home on? What were the sales of all agricultural products from this property?

What are the annual cost of utilities and fuels for this home?

If you pay rent, what is the monthly rent?

If you own this home, what is your mortgage?

If you own this home, do you have a second mortgage?

What were the real estate taxes on this property last year?

What was the annual payment for fire, hazard, and flood insurance last year?

What is the value of this property?

If this is a condominium, what is the monthly fee?

If this is a mobile home, what were the total monthly costs, including rent, fees, taxes, etc.?

[1]As of February, 1998. Some questions have been condensed by the author.

Glossary

apprentices Apprentices were bound by a contract to assist a craftsman (like a silversmith or a blacksmith) for a number of years in exchange for being taught the craft.

decennial Being done or occurring once every ten years.

discrimination To treat some people worse than others for reasons of race, religion, or national background.

ethnic A member of a minority group who may keep the customs, language, or views of that group.

federal budget The federal budget is the amount of money the United States government has or plans to spend in one year.

immigrate A person who comes from another country to establish permanent residence.

indentured servant One who by contract sold his or her services to a master for a certain number of years in exchange for the master's payment of passage to America and living expenses.

integrated Open to all people, no matter what their race, religion, or national background is.

internment camps Remote areas surrounded by barbed wire where Americans of Japanese background were forced to live during World War II when the U.S. government was at war with Germany and Japan.

literacy The ability to read and write.

market survey A set of questions that gathers information about people's preferences for products and services.

radical A person who wants extreme or rapid political change.

real estate Property in buildings or land.

register To sign up for, especially in order to vote.

repeal To cancel or eliminate.

standard of living The level of necessities and comforts a person or a group requires.

subscription The purchase ahead of time of future issues of a magazine or newspaper.

technology Scientific or technical knowledge.

Further Reading

Hakim, Joy. *The Story of US*, volumes 1–10. New York: Oxford University Press, 1994.

Bibliography

Alterman, Hyman. *Counting People: The Census in History*. New York: Harcourt Brace, 1969.

Anderson, Margo J. *The American Census: A Social History*. New Haven, CT: Yale University Press, 1988.

Bohme, Frederick and George Dailey. "1990 Census: The 21st Count of 'We The People'," *Social Education*, November/December, 1989.

Bohme, Frederick. "200 Years of Census Factfinding," *Social Education*, November/December, 1989.

Bryant, Barbara Everitt and William Dunn. *Moving Power and Money: The Politics of Census Taking*. Ithaca, NY: The New Strategist, 1995.

Campbell-Kelly, Martin and William Aspray. *Computer: A History of the Information Machine*. New York: Basic Books, 1996.

Cassedy, James. *Demography in Early America*. Cambridge, MA: Harvard University Press, 1969.

Christman, Margaret. *1846: Portrait of the Nation*. Washington, D.C.: Smithsonian Institution Press, 1996.

Clemence, Ted. *"Indians Not Taxed."* Bureau of the Census, 1981.

Eckler, A. Ross. *The Bureau of the Census*. New York: Praeger, 1972.

Ellis, Joseph J. *American Sphinx: The Character of Thomas Jefferson*. New York: Random House, 1996.

Goldston, Robert. *The Coming of the Civil War*. New York: Macmillan, 1972.

Higham, John. *Strangers in the Land: Patterns of American Nativism. 1860–1925*. New Brunswick, NJ: Rutgers University Press, 1988.

Johnson, Paul. *A History of the American People*, New York: HarperCollins, 1997.

Larkin, Jack. *The Reshaping of Everyday Life: 1790-1840*. New York: Harper-Collins, 1988.

McKay, Robert B. *Reapportionment: The Law and Politics of Equal Representation*. New York: Twentieth Century Fund, 1965.

McKay, Michael V. "Constitutional Implications of a Population Undercount: Making Sense of the Census Clause." *Georgetown Law Review*, vol. 69, pp. 1427–1463.

McPherson. *Battle Cry of Freedom: The Civil War Era*. New York: Oxford University Press, 1988.

Nugent, Walter. *Structures of American Social History*. Bloomington, IN: Indiana University Press, 1981.

Rossiter, William. *A Century of Population Growth*. U.S. Bureau of the Census, 1909.

Shannon, David. *The Twenties and Thirties* (vol. 2) Twentieth Century America series. Chicago: Rand McNally, 1977.

"200 Years of US Census Taking: Population and Housing Questions, 1790–1990." US Bureau of the Census, November, 1989.

Wright, Carroll and William Hunt. *History and Growth of the United States Census*. Washington, D.C.: Government Printing Office, 1900.

Index